on the radar

cool
brands

Liz Gogerly

Lerner Publications Company
Minneapolis

First American edition published in 2012 by Lerner Publishing Group, Inc. Published by arrangement with Wayland, a division of Hachette Children's Books

Lerner Publications Company
A division of Lerner Publishing Group, Inc.
241 First Avenue North
Minneapolis, MN U.S.A.

Website address: www.lernerbooks.com

Library of Congress Cataloging-in-Publication Data

Gogerly, Liz.
   Cool brands / by Liz Gogerly.
      p.   cm. — (On the radar: street style)
   Includes index.
   ISBN 978-0-7613-7770-2 (lib. bdg. : alk. paper)
   1. Brand-name products—Juvenile literature.
   2. Branding (Marketing)—Juvenile literature. I. Title.
   HD69.B7G64 2012
   658.8'27—dc23   2011023398

Manufactured in the United States of America
  – CG – 12/31/11

Acknowledgments: AP Photo/PRNewsFoto/MilkPEP, 3; Corbis: Cynthia Hart Designer 8, Rick Friedman 6, Sara De Boer/Retna Ltd 14-15; Getty Images: William King cover; iStock: Brandon Alms 10br, Skip O'Donnell 12cl, 10l, ollo 6br, Shane Shaw 6tr, Todor cvetkov 3, 11, Mathias Wilson 7; © Levi Strauss & Co. Archives, San Francisco 12t; Rex: BDG 23; Shutterstock: aGinger 2r, 4-5, Galina Barskaya 12b, BMCL 20, Eric Broder Van Dyke 9t, clarusvisus 17, Songquan Deng 2b, 30b, ecxcn 2-3, 28-29, gary 718 1, 2t, 19, Iculig 22, Stuart Miles 31b, Monkey Business images 31t, Tupungato 30cl; Stocks Taylor Benson: 24-25, 25bl, 25bc, 25br.

Main body text set in
Helvetica Neue LT Std 13/15.5.
Typeface provided by Adobe Systems.

cover stories

thepeople

theart

thetalk

Coca-Cola, Aston Martin *(right)*, and the iPhone are all cool brands. Year after year, they are listed in surveys of the best brands. What is it about these brands that makes people want them so badly? Are they really that special, or is it just clever marketing?

COOL BRANDS!

Branding

The success of any product relies on many factors, but when it comes to selling things, branding is right up there at the top. The brand of a product or company is its identity. It's what we think when we hear the name. The brand identity is made up of the name, the logo, the image, and the marketing of the product or company. When people hear "iPhone," they already know things about that product. Many people will think, "I'd love one of those." That proves that Apple, the company that makes the iPhone, has its branding just right!

Being the best

What makes certain brands cooler than others? In 2010 British car manufacturer Aston Martin beat the iPhone to number one on the BrandZ Top 100 in the United States. In recent years, the iPhone had topped most people's wish lists. So what caused this change in chart position? The answer could be that most people can't own the product. More and more people own an iPhone, making it less exclusive. Meanwhile, Aston Martin cars are so expensive that most people can only dream of owning one.

Face of a brand

For extra selling power, some brands identify famous people with their product. For example, pop music superstar Lady Gaga gets paid extra to feature certain products, such as Monster headphones and MAC makeup, in her music videos. When fans see Gaga using these products, they want to buy them to be like her. Megastars Jay-Z and Justin Bieber have also developed and become their own brands.

BRAND CHAT

For the coolest brand lingo, check out our On the Radar guide!

billboard
a large board, usually on the streets, on which advertisements are posted

graphic design
the creation of elements, such as typography or images, that communicate a message or brand

packaging
the wrapping and boxes in which a product is sold

brand loyalty
a person's commitment to buying only one brand or product

exclusive
something that is available only to a limited set of people

retail
the direct sale of goods in a store to customers

consumer
a person who buys and uses a product or a service

limited edition
something made in only a small number

slogan
a phrase expressing the aims of a business and repeated in advertising and promotion of the company's products

logo
symbols, letters, or a graphic representation of a company name or trademark

trademark
symbolized by the logo ™, a sign that tells the consumer a product or brand name is owned by the manufacturer

marketing
the methods, such as advertising, used to tell a consumer about a product

typeface
a specific style of lettering; also called typography

mass-produce
to manufacture goods in large quantities in a factory

GLOSSARY

brainwashing
using techniques such as advertising to make a person believe something

debit cards
plastic cards used as a method of payment. The money is taken from a person's bank account automatically.

denim
a strong cotton fabric used to make jeans and other clothing

fashionista
someone who wears the latest fashions

generic
shared by, typical of, or relating to a group of similar things

iconic
easy to recognize

Industrial Revolution
the period of time from the eighteenth to the nineteenth centuries during which mass production in factories replaced the man-made production of goods

innovative
using new methods and ideas

manufacturers
companies that produce goods in large numbers

netting (a profit)
earning or making a clear profit after all deductions have been made

phenomenon
something that is impressive and extraordinary

prodigy
a person with exceptional or extraordinary talents at an early age

survey
a report or a study

virtual
online

BRAND-NEW START

Brands surround us. It's hard to imagine a world without the marketing and branding of products. But branding is something that really took off only in the second half of the nineteenth century.

Coca-Cola promoted its brand with clever advertising that lifted the product above the competition.

All change

During the Industrial Revolution (around 1750–1900), great changes took place in all aspects of life. This was caused by the growth of factories and of mass-produced goods. Until then, most people had been used to a limited selection of locally made products. After the Industrial Revolution, they were presented with choices.

Branding begins

Meanwhile, the manufacturers wanted their products to stand out. When they transported their goods from factories, they used a hot iron to mark the factory brand on their products. The term *branded* came from this practice. Some successful brands that we recognize, including Kellogg's, Campbell's, Coca-Cola, and Levi's, were among those great nineteenth-century manufacturers. These companies have built a brand loyalty that has lasted for well over a century.

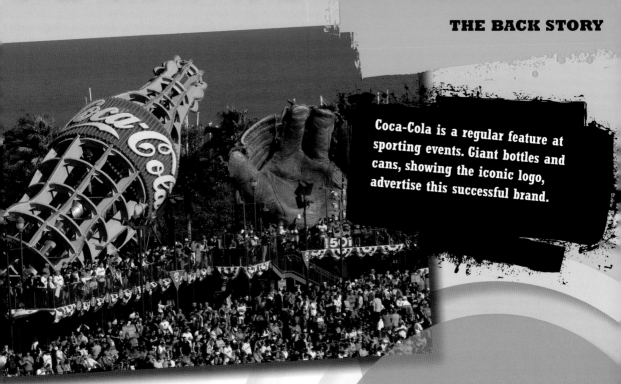

Coca-Cola is a regular feature at sporting events. Giant bottles and cans, showing the iconic logo, advertise this successful brand.

Cool and fizzy

Coca-Cola is possibly the best-known brand of all time. The soft-drink company was founded in 1892 in Atlanta, Georgia. Its famous fizzy beverage is available in more than 200 countries. Coca-Cola, or Coke, also has one of the most recognizable logos on the planet!

Lasting logo

The Coca-Cola logo has hardly changed since it was first designed. The original typeface of Coca-Cola resembled the formal handwriting style of the late 1800s. And it has stood the test of time—appearing on bottles, cans, glasses, billboards, and signs.

The branding timeline

- 1853 Levi Strauss, the owner of the clothing company that launched Levi's jeans, opens his first business in San Francisco, California.
- 1894 Milton Hershey begins making dark, sweet chocolates. He would later switch to creating milk chocolate and make a fortune.
- 1896 Henry Ford test-drove the Quadricycle, his first gas-powered car. Within 10 years, his Ford Motor Company was churning out affordable cars.
- 1906 The Battle Creek Toasted Corn Flake Company was founded in Michigan. Its name was changed to the Kellogg Company in 1922.

BRANDING COMES OF AGE

Brands have moved on since the 1800s. Coca-Cola is one of the most valuable brands in the world. But in the twenty-first century, there are more brands than ever. Toys R Us, Barbie, and Lego show that kids become aware of branding from an early age.

Branding is an everyday part of our culture—whether you are into Barbie or Nintendo. Probably, you have bought a branded product at some point!

Twenty-first-century movers

As they grow older, kids might switch to sports or technology brands such as Nike or Nintendo. Around the early teenage years, more sophisticated brands begin to take over, such as Apple with its iPhone, iPod, and iPad. And that is just the beginning—the brands just keep on coming.

Google it!

The Google brand is a Web winner. Founded in 1998, the company offers users a free search engine that is the most popular in the world. By 2002 the words *to Google* had passed into everyday speech. If anyone has a question about anything, the common response is "Google it!"

On average, the Google website has over 2 billion hits every day!

Visual punch

Great brands have something in common. They have built a strong relationship with the customer. They have done this because they represent excellent products and have moved with the times. The brands are also successful because they are seen in all the right places. Advertising on billboards, in shops, in magazines, on television, and in movie theaters keeps brands in the public eye.

Surfing to success

In the twenty-first century, the big brands target people browsing the Internet. Meanwhile, the Internet has helped to make many brands successful. The retailer Amazon and the social-networking sites Facebook, MySpace, Twitter, and Google+ have all made their names on the Web.

TWO HORSE BRAND
TRADE MARK
LEVI STRAUSS & CO.

LIFESTYLE LABELS

Nike

Nike, as worn by Spanish tennis star Rafael Nadal

One of the most important parts of running a successful business is figuring out how to sell your brand. These days, businesses have noticed a trend. Customers want to be like athletes! By buying brands that athletes market or wear, consumers are able to be like their heroes. So what tools do these companies use to sell their stuff?

The face

The right face makes the right slogan even more powerful. Some slogans are so catchy that they have become part of our everyday lives. "Got Milk?" has been plastered across billboards and magazines for years. It got an athletic spin when Super Bowl MVP Aaron Rodgers *(right)* and soccer great David Beckham sported milk mustaches.

The logo

Nike considers itself the leading designer of clothing and accessories for athletes. The company is all about cool clothes that keep you just as comfortable working out as hanging out. The company's logo— the famous Nike swoosh—is somewhere between a check mark and a wing. The wing comes from Nike, the Greek goddess of victory. The use of the logo and the goddess's name bring to mind the self-confidence that comes from winning—and from wearing Nike clothing, of course.

The name

Clothing brand Levi's appeals to kids who want comfortable, fashionable clothes. But the brand has its humble beginnings in the California gold rush of the mid-1800s. Gold miners needed jeans that were strong and comfortable enough for their daily work. Ever since, the brand name has appealed to a wide range of people, including athletes and celebrities. The name Levi's is simple, trustworthy, and American—just like the jeans.

Game-winning pass.
Ever since I was a kid, my mom and coach taught me that to play my best, I need to fuel up to play 60. And one of the best ways to do that is with milk. Even now that I'm a Super Bowl champion, milk's still part of my game plan. Make it part of yours.

got milk?
whymilk.com/aaronrodgers

Got Milk?

BRAND BECKHAM

THE STATS

Name: David Robert Joseph Beckham (nickname Becks)
Born: May 2, 1975
Place of birth: London, England
Nationality: British
Job: Soccer player, model, and UNICEF ambassador

THE STATS

Name: Victoria Caroline Beckham (nickname Posh Spice)
Born: April 17, 1974
Place of birth: Essex, England
Nationality: British
Job: Fashion designer, singer-songwriter, and model

Posh and Becks

From the early days of their romance, David and Victoria were always in the news. There were plenty of Posh and Becks tales to tell. In 1999 they had their first child, and just a few months later, they were married during a lavish fairy-tale wedding. Next, they moved into a large, stately home, nicknamed Beckingham Palace!

Style icon

When her music career as a member of the Spice Girls ended, Victoria launched a line of sunglasses, a range of denim clothing, and a his and hers fragrance line called Intimately Beckham. In 2008 she stunned the fashion world with her 1950s-inspired collection of clothing. The Victoria Beckham Collection has earned her praise from the fashion and celebrity worlds.

The soccer hero

David's talent on the soccer field has earned him hero status. As one of the world's most famous athletes, he has the power to sell anything from sports equipment and underwear. David also goes to war-torn countries to spend time with troops.

Brand it like Beckham

David and Victoria have been in the spotlight for more than a decade. In that time, they have moved on from being colorful celebrities to mega marketing tools. These days Brand Beckham is a power to be reckoned with. As well as raising money for charities and for the Olympic Games, the brand has the power to sell just about anything.

BECKHAM

"The thing that I really care about is making the world more open and connected," Zuckerberg says.

THE FACEBOOK BILLIONAIRE

At the start of 2011, Facebook had more than 600 million active users. By 2012 this number could reach one billion—one-sixth of the world's population. Facebook is a social-networking phenomenon, but who is the brain behind this famous brand?

Information-age genius

Facebook cofounder and president is programming prodigy Mark Zuckerberg. At Harvard, Mark was a typical student who liked a good prank. One weekend in 2003, he set up an Internet site called Facemash, onto which he uploaded photographs of other Harvard students. Visitors to the site got to vote for the best-looking students! By Monday the college had shut down the site. Facemash was no more, but it sparked the idea for something big.

Network whirlwind

Fast-forward to February 2004, when Zuckerberg launched Facebook. Initially, the site was meant for Harvard students. It was a virtual meeting place where they could learn more about one another's lives. The idea quickly caught on, and Zuckerberg expanded the site to other colleges. By summer 2004, Zuckerberg and some fellow students set up their first office in California. There was no turning back. Zuckerberg dropped out of Harvard to concentrate on developing Facebook. His dream was to offer people a limitless way to connect with one another.

Facing the future

By 2007 Facebook was a global website with more than 150,000 people signing up each day. With Facebook translated into more than 100 languages and its popularity growing worldwide, Zuckerberg's dream is definitely on track.

HELLO KITTY

The cat that got the cash

Who's that girl?

Hello Kitty is the cute cat that is loved around the world. Her face appears on everything from backpacks, watches, and lunch boxes to paper and pens. Little girls love Hello Kitty cuddly toys, while older girls are happy to wear Hello Kitty T-shirts. She may look sweet, but Hello Kitty is one of the most successful brands on the planet, netting between $1 billion and $5 billion a year.

The cat enters

This little ball of branding magic was created in Tokyo, Japan, in 1974 by Sanrio, a small company that produced gifts and accessories. Sanrio asked its designer Yuko Shimizu to come up with a character to appeal to the preteen market. She sketched Kitty White. Kitty made her very first appearance on a plastic coin purse.

The cat with nine lives

Hello Kitty has traveled farther than her wildest dreams. By 1976 she had made it to the United States, where the brand has expanded into more than 4,000 shops. Eva Air, a Taiwanese airline, adopted Kitty in 2005. She decorates the flight attendants' uniforms. In 2009 the Bank of America offered its customers debit cards bearing the pretty Kitty face.

What's the secret?

Clever marketing means that the Hello Kitty brand can be seen almost everywhere. However, the company produces some products in small numbers to boost their appeal. Part of Kitty's popularity comes from the simplicity of the brand. Because she has a strong image, she has been able to move with the times and appear on a wide range of products. This lovable cat spans the age range and has been spotted on wine bottles and even in Nintendo DS games. Hello Kitty is predictable, yet she keeps people guessing—a very clever brand (and Kitty!) indeed.

Hello Kitty flies into New York City—as a giant balloon!

Career highlights

2005 *Hello Kitty: Roller Rescue,* an action adventure game, was released on Xbox, GameCube, and PlayStation 2.

2008 A Hello Kitty–themed maternity hospital opened in Taiwan—everything from the nurses' uniforms to the bedsheets sported the famous cat!

2009 iPhone released the highly successful game *Hello Kitty: Parachute Paradise.*

MONEY DOES GROW ON TREES

CIRCA
WORTH MORE

TOLL FREE 800 8 8490
WWW.CIRCAJEWELS.COM
THE SOLE INTERNATIONAL JEWELRY BUYING FIRM

Career highlights

1976 Apple I goes on the market.

1984 The first Macs are for sale.

1998 iMacs transform the personal computer (PC) industry.

2001 Apple opened its first two retail stores, called Apple Stores, in Virginia and California.

2003 The company launched its online music shop, iTunes.

2008 It opened the App Store, selling applications such as games and business tools.

2011 Apple launches iPad 2, which is faster than the original iPad and features two cameras.

THE STATS

Name: Apple Inc.
Born: April 1, 1976
Place of birth: Steve Jobs's bedroom, Cupertino, California

When Apple opened its first Australian store in 2008, crowds lined up outside for over 24 hours!

APPLE INC.

The Apple of our "i"

Computer whiz kids

Apple Computer Inc. was the brainchild of Steve Jobs and Steve Wozniak. In 1972 the two men met while working for the Internet technology company Hewlett-Packard. They discovered they both shared an interest in PCs. In 1975 they turned their interest into a project and began work on their first PC, the Apple I. In 1976 Ron Wayne, a colleague of Jobs's, joined them and Apple Computer Inc. was founded.

Apple Computer struggled early on due to lack of funds. Amazingly, the team managed to assemble 50 Apple I PCs in just 10 days. However, Wayne believed the business was too risky and sold his share of the company after 12 days. (His share would be worth over $3 billion today!)

Byte of the Apple

Jobs and Wozniak were determined to persevere with the company. Their determination paid off. By the end of the 1970s, Apple was instantly recognizable by its distinctive logo. It also employed a large team of designers. The company had an efficient production line that created thousands of Apple II computers, one of the first micro PCs to achieve great success.

In 1984 Apple released the Macintosh. In 1998 it launched the iMac, the fastest-selling PC in history. Apple's PowerBooks and iBooks came on the market. They were sleeker and faster with each new model.

Top tech

In the 2000s, Apple switched its focus to mobile electronic devices. In 2001 it released the iPod, a palm-sized digital music player that swiftly became the best-selling portable music player ever.

The year 2007 was another turning point in Apple's history as the company changed its name to Apple Inc. and released the revolutionary iPhone and the iPod Touch. Then, in 2010, Apple launched the iPad, a portable, handheld media tablet that gave users access to the Internet and a whole host of newspapers, ebooks, films, and music, as well as Apple's App Store.

Big Apple

By 2012 Apple was one of the most popular cool brands of all time. The only worm in the Apple is what impact the resignation of Jobs in 2011 will have on the company.

BATTLE OF THE BOOTS

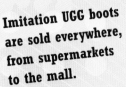

The ugg boot has been around for decades, but in the mid-2000s, it stepped into the limelight. Seen on the feet of supermodels and celebrities, the boot became a fashionista must-have!

Imitation UGG boots are sold everywhere, from supermarkets to the mall.

Looking sheepish

In the past, Australian and New Zealand sheep shearers wrapped sheepskin around their legs to keep warm. They called their crudely fashioned legwear uggs, thought to be from the word *ugly*. In the 1960s, Australian surfers began wearing uggs. And in the 1970s, U.S. surfers followed suit. A California surfer named Brian Smith started UGG Holdings Inc., exporting boots from Australia and New Zealand.

Terms and trademarks

In the beginning, *uggs* was a generic term for sheepskin boots made in Australia and New Zealand. This meant that anyone producing the boots in those countries could call them uggs. In 1995 the U.S. company Deckers Outdoor Corporation bought UGG Holdings Inc. In 1996 Deckers bought the U.S. trademark (legal ownership) for the UGG Australia brand.

Tug of the ugg

Deckers hit the big time in the mid-2000s. This should have been good news for ugg producers everywhere. But then Deckers pulled the plug on anyone else calling their boots uggs. Deckers claimed that UGG was a trademark and that only it had the right to use the name. Australian and New Zealand manufacturers were furious. They battled to keep the ugg name for all. In 2006 the Australian and New Zealand manufacturers finally won the right to use ugg in their own countries.

Style wars

Deckers is still fighting to stay stylish. In 2010 it employed famous shoe designer Jimmy Choo to give the boots a makeover. The limited-edition boots featured animal prints, fringing, and studs. The battle for the brand may have ended, but the style wars have only just begun.

By the mid-2000s, celebrities such as Jennifer Lopez *(above)*, Kate Moss, and Madonna had helped to jump-start a trend for comfy UGG boots.

JOHN BENSON

John Benson is one of the founding members of Stocks Taylor Benson, a commercial graphic design company. This team of designers has worked with some of the coolest brands, including Quiksilver, Speedo, Office Depot, and Black & Decker. Here John tells On the Radar what makes a cool brand!

What makes a successful brand?

A successful brand is so much more than one product, one logo, or one piece of packaging. It's about the complete picture. A winning brand is about the whole company and everything surrounding it. It's about the people working for the company, the design of the products, and where the products are sold. It's even about how the telephone is answered!

How do you create a best-selling brand?

Brands that do well focus on their brand values—the things that set them apart from their competitors. Brands that fail lose sight of their core message and try too hard to appeal to everyone.

What makes an eye-catching logo?

A great logo is not just about making a pretty picture. The logo should be clear and simple. There should be logic to the logo and a really strong reason why it was designed that way.

What is your best advice for creating a winning brand?

My number one tip is to keep things clear. Your branding should be easily understood, and it should be obvious at whom it is aimed. If it's a unique product, then this should be made clear. It doesn't matter whether the product is funky and innovative or steeped in tradition. The branding should be straightforward.

What is the story behind the Nike logo?

It was created in 1971 by a U.S. graphic design student named Carolyn Davidson. Philip Knight, the owner of Blue Ribbon Sports, asked her to design a logo for a new sports footwear range he was about to launch, called Nike. Carolyn came up with the now-famous swoosh symbol, which represents a wing of the Greek goddess Nike. The logo and the footwear were so successful that the company changed its name to Nike, Inc., in 1978 . . . and the rest is history.

What is it about your job that you enjoy?

Every time I see something that we've designed, I still get a real tingle inside. It could be some packaging in a store, an advertisement in a newspaper, or a logo going by on the side of a truck . . . . I love it!

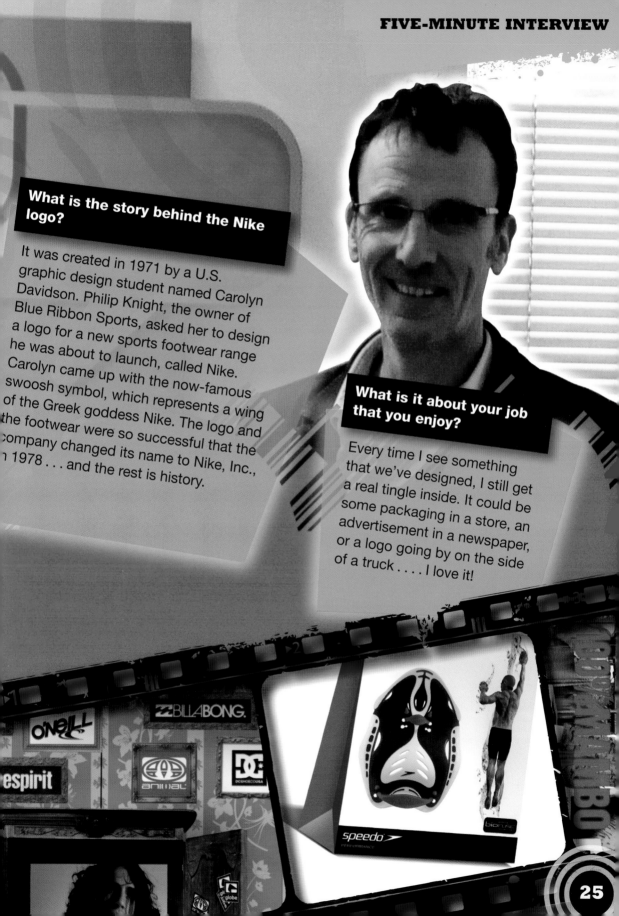

LOGO DESIGN

Your logo should be distinctive and relevant. But before you start designing, make sure you understand your market by asking questions and listening to the answers.

You will need:

- paper • pencils • markers
- imagination and creativity
- computer software (optional)

1 Collect examples of the kinds of graphics that you think a target audience is drawn to.

2 Think about how the name of your brand might lend itself to an image that you can use alongside the word.

3 Write down any idea that come into your head. Don't spend too long on each idea. Try to come up with as many as possible.

4

Take your favorite ideas and fine-tune them. Maybe two of the ideas could be joined together into one great logo?

5

You may want to use computer software to draw the logo neatly and to apply color. Consider which colors would suit your logo. You might even decide that black and white works best.

on the
ɔɒdɒr

Got it?

Show your logo to friends, and note how they react. Are those friends in the target audience? If so, are they attracted to it? If they are, then you've designed a successful logo!

BRAND BUSTERS!

19 BILLION

The number of Lego bricks produced each year!

5th

The country's population ranking if the users of Facebook were the population of a country!

3 MILLION

The number of iPads sold worldwide within the first 80 days of its launch in April 2010.

80

The percentage of Nintendo DS owners between the ages of 8 and 16.

700
BILLION

The number of
minutes spent on
Facebook by its
users each month.

1.7
BILLION

The number of servings of
Coca-Cola sold each
day around the world.

65
MILLION

The number of tweets
generated every day
on Twitter.

124

The number of available
languages for Google, the
most used search engine
in the world.

1
BILLION

The number of Barbie
dolls sold since their
creation in 1959.

COOL CULTURE OR GREED?

FOR

Many people love cool brands and do not mind paying extra for them. They believe branded items are better than "no-name" ones. They say:

1. Brands say a lot about a person. Cool, branded products signify success and imply that the owner knows what they want and how to get it.
2. People trust the brands they know and see advertised a lot.
3. Some brands go way beyond cool! When a person buys these brands, they know that the goods are innovative and offer something different from the other "me-too" companies.
4. People like the exclusivity of luxury brands. They want the things that other people cannot afford. It makes them feel like a million bucks!
5. Buying into a brand can make young people feel accepted and part of the club.

However, other people think that buying top brands is unnecessary or just plain wrong! They say:

AGAINST

1. Cool brands focus on the marketing and branding of a product so much that they sometimes forget about the product itself.
2. It is all a con! People who think that luxury brands are better are just being tricked. For example, handbags that are said to be handmade in Italy are sometimes partly made in China in the same factories where "no-name" bags are also made.
3. Some brands do well just because large companies are able to fund glitzy advertising campaigns. Advertising is just brainwashing.
4. People do not like the effect of branding on young people. This desire to own expensive items creates a must-have mentality and can lead to debt or even crime.
5. Buying into brands can make those who cannot afford cool brands feel left out or inferior.

RIGHT OR WRONG?

Cool or not? Buying into a cool brand gives people a certain social status. It can give them a sense of satisfaction that they have bought the very best product available. But if this means that people resort to crime or get into debt to buy the brand, the clever marketing is only adding to their own—and society's—problems.

GET MORE INFO

Books

Fuller, Donna Jo. *The Stock Market*. Minneapolis: Lerner Publications Company, 2006.

Gilman, Laura Anne. *Economics*. Minneapolis: Lerner Publications Company, 2006.

McGowan, Eileen Nixon, and Nancy Lagow Dumas. *Stock Market Smart*. Millbrook Press, 2002.

McPherson, Stephanie Sammartino. *Levi Strauss*. Minneapolis: Lerner Publications Company, 2007.

Sutcliffe, Jane. *Milton Hershey*. Minneapolis: Lerner Publications Company, 2004.

Thomas, Keltie. *The Kids Guide to Money Cents*. Tonawanda, NY: Kids Can Press, 2004.

Zuehlke, Jeffrey. *Henry Ford*. Minneapolis: Lerner Publications Company, 2007.

Websites

BrandZ
http://www.millwardbrown.com/ BrandZ/default.aspx
This site provides annual lists of the coolest and most successful brands in the world.

Forbes
http://www.forbes.com/lists/
Check out some of *Forbes*'s famous lists, where the most powerful celebrities, richest people, and most successful businesses are ranked.

Gazillionaire
http://www.gazillionaire.com/ gazillionaire.php
This is an intergalactic game of building your own brand.

INDEX